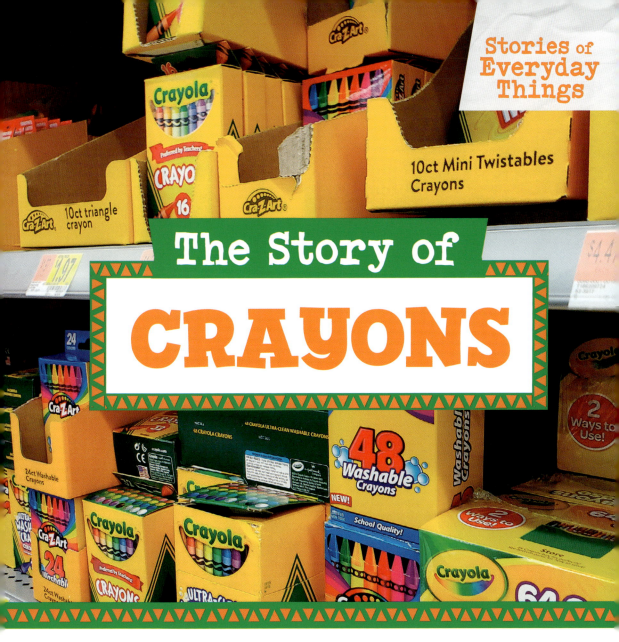

Stories of Everyday Things

The Story of CRAYONS

by Mae Respicio

PEBBLE
a capstone imprint

Published by Pebble, an imprint of Capstone
1710 Roe Crest Drive, North Mankato, Minnesota 56003
capstonepub.com

Copyright © 2025 by Capstone. All rights reserved. No part of this publication may be reproduced in whole or in part, or stored in a retrieval system, or transmitted in any form or by any means, electronic, mechanical, photocopying, recording, or otherwise, without written permission of the publisher.

Library of Congress Cataloging-in-Publication Data is available on the Library of Congress website.
ISBN: 9780756582012 (hardcover)
ISBN: 9780756582098 (paperback)
ISBN: 9780756582074 (ebook PDF)

Summary: Red, blue, purple, green—crayons come in a rainbow of colors! But when were crayons first discovered? How have they changed throughout time? And how are they made today? Learn the answers to these questions and more in this informational book all about crayons.

Editorial Credits
Editor: Alison Deering; Designer: Jaime Willems; Media Researcher: Jo Miller; Production Specialist: Whitney Schaefer

Image Credits

Alamy: dpa picture alliance, 15, GL Archive, 11; Getty Images: leolintang, Back Cover, 27, Melinda Podor, 25, William Thomas Cain, 17, 18, 19, 20; Shutterstock: Aleksandr Medvedkov, 21, Alexander_Safonov, 28, Alexxndr, 24, Everett Collection, 9, fotosen55, 10, Gorodenkoff, 22, Hasnuddin, 5, kosolovskyy, 16, Nai_Pisage, Cover (loose crayons), Pascal RATEAU, 6, photogal, 12, Sstudi, Cover (box of crayons), Steve Lovegrove, 13, The Image Party, 1, 23, Vladimir Melnik, 8, Yury Birukov, 7

Design Elements: Shutterstock: Luria, Pooretat moonsana

Any additional websites and resources referenced in this book are not maintained, authorized, or sponsored by Capstone. All product and company names are trademarks™ or registered® trademarks of their respective holders.

Printed in the United States   5997

Table of Contents

All About Crayons 4

History of Crayons 6

Modern Crayons 10

Crayon-Making Magic 14

How Crayons Reach Us 20

Crayons Today 24

    Make Your Own Crayons! 28

    Glossary 30

    Read More 31

    Internet Sites 31

    Index 32

    About the Author 32

Words in **bold** appear in the glossary.

All About Crayons

They come in lots of beautiful colors. They help us create art. They help us have fun! What are they? Crayons!

Are crayons just for kids? Not at all. Anyone can use and enjoy them. You just need an imagination. All around the world, people know and love crayons. But how did they become an everyday thing?

History of Crayons

Crayons were not invented by just one person. Throughout history, people have used objects from nature to make art. Some examples include berries, clay, animal fat, crushed rocks, and plants. These materials acted as **pigments** or colors.

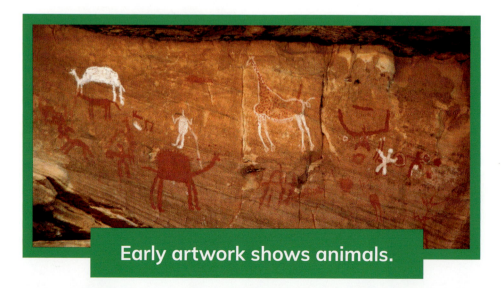

Early artwork shows animals.

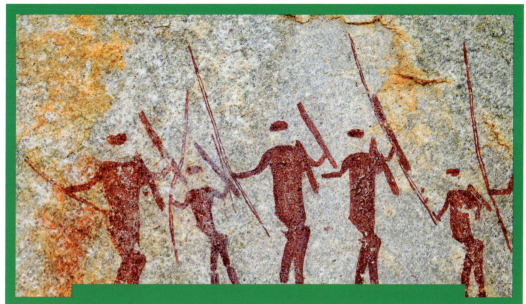
Ancient drawings also show hunters.

The word *crayon* comes from the French word *craie*. It means *chalk*. One of the oldest crayons in the world was discovered in England. It was a piece of reddish-brown **ochre**. In 2008 it was tested. It was found to be 10,000 years old!

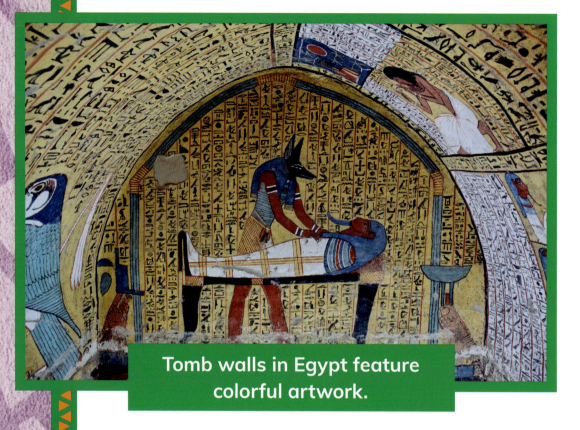

Tomb walls in Egypt feature colorful artwork.

Ancient Egyptians also used a type of crayon. They mixed **beeswax** with pigments. This made colored sticks. They used them to draw on **tombs** and temples. Crayon-like drawings from 100 CE have been found in Egypt.

In the 1500s, an artist named Leonardo da Vinci used a type of crayon called **pastels**. These were pigments mixed with things like fig juice or fish glue.

Leonardo da Vinci

In the 1700s, some artists used crayons made from clay. This type of crayon was the **Conté crayon**.

Modern Crayons

In the 1800s, crayons only came in one color. Black. These were not good for kids. They were made from charcoal and oil. These were **toxic** materials.

charcoal drawing sticks

In 1885, two cousins started a company in New York City. Edwin Binney and C. Harold Smith wanted to make crayons safe for kids. They invented a new type of crayon. They made theirs with melted wax and pigments.

Edwin Binney

In 1903, Binney and Smith launched their first crayons. Binney's wife Alice also helped. She was a former schoolteacher. She suggested making the crayons more affordable. She also came up with the name—Crayola. It means *oily chalk* in French.

a five-cent coin

Crayola crayons changed how people made art. They were smooth and nontoxic. There were only eight colors in the first box! But they were less expensive. They only cost five cents. More people could use them.

Crayon-Making Magic

Crayons can be made in different ways. Some people make their own. Ashrita Furman holds the record for making the world's tallest crayon. It measures more than 17 feet (5 meters) tall. That is taller than a giraffe!

But most crayons sold in stores are made in factories. How? With the help of people and machines.

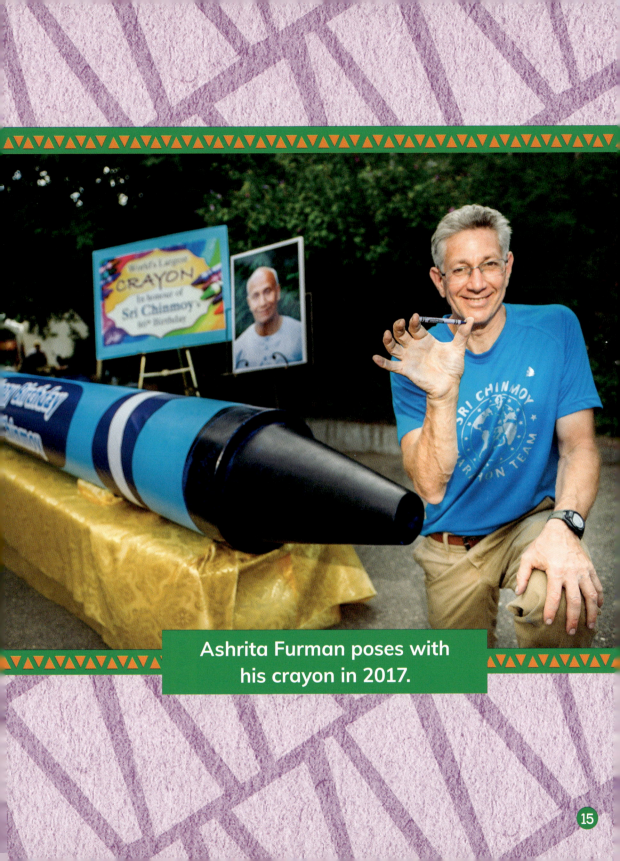
Ashrita Furman poses with his crayon in 2017.

beeswax

Crayons have two main ingredients. The first is wax. There are different kinds of wax, including paraffin or beeswax. Wax is melted down. This makes the base.

The other ingredient is pigment. Pigments are usually powders. A factory worker pours them from a big bag. They are mixed into the wax base. Mixing them in exact amounts makes different **hues**.

A worker adds pigment to a wax base.

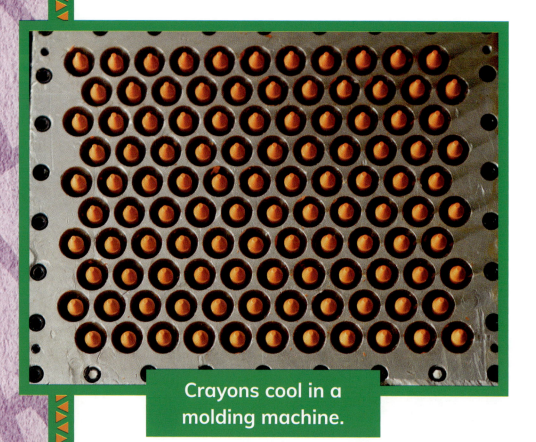

Crayons cool in a molding machine.

What happens next? The liquid mixture is poured into **molds**. These give crayons their classic shape. The mixture needs time to cool. It takes around four to seven minutes.

Finally, the mixture is solid. Each crayon is checked. Some factories even use metal detectors. They make sure nothing is in the crayons that should not be.

A worker checks and packages crayons.

How Crayons Reach Us

Do you love opening a fresh box of crayons? Many people do. But how do crayons get into your hands? First, they are packaged in the factories where they are made. Then, they are sent to warehouses.

Boxes of crayons are prepared for shipping in a factory.

Are the crayons ready to reach you? Almost. Next up? **Distribution**. That is the way something is delivered.

Trucks wait at a distribution center.

To get to stores, crayons must go on a journey. **Wholesalers** distribute the crayons. They supply them to stores and online shops.

Some crayons go far. The boxes are loaded onto trucks, trains, or ships. They are delivered to stores. The boxes are put on display.

The last step? The one you have waited for. Unboxing and coloring! Choose your colors. Let your creativity soar. Time to make your art and share it!

Crayons Today

Today, crayons have come even further. Now they have a digital twist. There are apps to use virtual crayons. You can have many colors at your fingertips. They never run out.

Other crayons are eco-friendly. They are made with soybeans or beeswax. Some are made of recycled crayons. This makes them better for the environment.

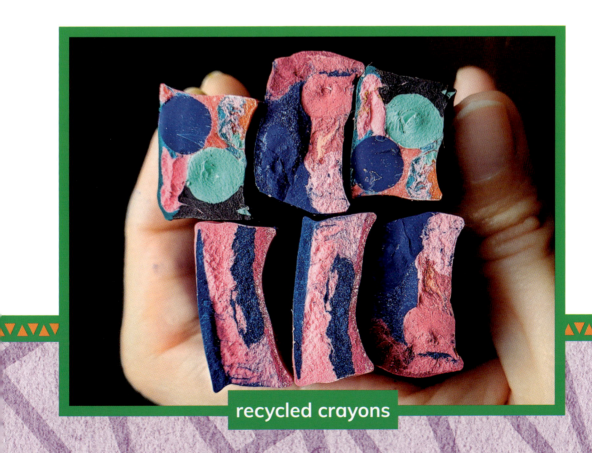

recycled crayons

How do people all over the world celebrate crayons? By drawing! There is even a National Crayon Day. It is celebrated on March 31.

Crayons bring many things into our everyday lives. Art. Creativity. Most of all? Joy. People love the fun they bring.

Make Your Own Crayons!

Have you ever wanted to make your own crayons? You can, by recycling old ones! This activity will need a grown-up's help.

What You Need:

- old crayons
- cupcake tins or oven-safe molds
- cooking spray
- oven mitts

What You Do:

1. With a grown-up's help, preheat the oven to 250°F (121°C).

2. Peel the labels off your crayons. Break them into smaller pieces. This will help them melt faster.

3. Spray your cupcake tins or molds with cooking spray. This will keep the crayons from sticking as they melt.

4. Place the broken crayons in the tins or molds. You can use whatever colors you like.

5. Ask a grown-up to help you place the crayons in the oven. Bake them for 15 minutes or until completely melted.

6. Using oven mitts, carefully remove the crayons from the oven. Be careful. The wax is very hot.

7. Let the crayons cool. Then pop them out and start coloring!

Glossary

beeswax (BEEZ-waks)—a yellow substance bees make to create honeycombs where they store honey

Conté crayon (KAWN-te KREY-on)—a type of crayon made from graphite or charcoal mixed with clay

distribution (dis-tri-BYOO-shun)—the act or process of giving out or delivering something

hue (HYOO)—a color or variation of a color

mold (MOHLD)—a model of an object

ochre (OH-ker)—a type of rock, usually red or yellow in color, that can be used as a pigment

pastel (pa-STEL)—a type of crayon made of ground color turned into a paste

pigment (PIG-muhnt)—a substance that gives something a particular color when it is present in it or is added to it

tomb (TOOM)—a room or building that holds a dead body

toxic (TOK-sik)—poisonous

wholesaler (HOHL-seyl-er)—a person whose business buys many goods and sells them in smaller amounts

Read More

Biebow, Natascha. *The Crayon Man: The True Story of the Invention of Crayola Crayons.* Boston: Houghton Mifflin Harcourt, 2019.

Hansen, Grace. *How Is a Crayon Made?* Minneapolis: Abdo Kids, 2018.

Neddo, Nick. *The Organic Artist for Kids: A DIY Guide to Making Your Own Eco-Friendly Art Supplies from Nature.* Beverly, MA: Quarry Books, 2020.

Internet Sites

Easy Science for Kids: Crayons
easyscienceforkids.com/crayons/

Kiddle: Crayon Facts for Kids
kids.kiddle.co/Crayon

Time for Kids: Welcome to the Crayola Factory!
timeforkids.com/g2/welcome-crayola-factory/

Index

ancient crayons, 6, 7, 8, 9

Binney, Alice, 12

Binney, Edwin, 11, 12

charcoal, 10

colors, 4, 6, 10, 13, 17, 23, 24

Conté crayon, 9

cost, 12, 13

Crayola, 12, 13

da Vinci, Leonardo, 9

distribution, 21, 22

factories, 14, 17, 19, 20

Furman, Ashrita, 14–15

National Crayon Day, 26

ochre, 7

pigments, 6, 8–9, 11, 17

records, 14

recycled crayons, 25

Smith, C. Harold, 11, 12

virtual crayons, 24

warehouses, 20

wax, 8, 11, 16–17, 25

About the Author

Mae Respicio is a nonfiction writer and middle-grade author whose novel, *The House That Lou Built*, won an Asian/Pacific American Libraries Association Honor Award and was an NPR Best Book. Mae lives with her family in California and some of her favorite everyday things include books, beaches, and ube ice cream.